THE ANAYA **SUN SIGN** *COMPANIONS*

ARIES

21 March-20 April

CELESTINE O'RYAN

ANAYA PUBLISHERS LIMITED
LONDON

First published in Great Britain in 1991 by
Anaya Publishers Ltd., Strode House, 44-50 Osnaburgh Street, London NW1 3ND

Copyright © Anaya Publishers Ltd 1991

ASTROLOGICAL CONSULTANT Jan Kurrels

Managing Editor	Judy Martin
Art Director	Nigel Osborne
Designers	Sally Stockwell
	Anne Clue
Illustrators	Marion Appleton
	David Ashby
	Lorraine Harrison
	Tony Masero
Indexer	Peter Barber

British Library Cataloguing in Publication Data
O'Ryan, Celestine
    Aries. – (Anaya sun sign companions).
    1. Astrology
    I. Title
    133.52
    ISBN 1-85470-050-2

TYPESET IN GREAT BRITAIN BY MIDFORD TYPESETTING LTD, LONDON
COLOUR ORIGINATION IN SINGAPORE BY COLUMBIA OFFSET LTD
PRINTED IN SINGAPORE BY TIMES OFFSET LTD

CONTENTS

21 MARCH - 20 APRIL

ARIES

Most people know their own sun sign, and you know that yours is Aries, but do you appreciate its full impact on every area of your life? Your Sun Sign Companion *is a guide to the many pleasures and preferences that are specific to you as an Arian subject. Your personality profile is here – and much more. You can find out not only where you fit into the grand astrological scheme and the ways the other zodiac signs connect with your own, but also discover the delights of the Arian foods that are your special delicacies; the plants that you should grow in your garden to enhance your Arian moods; the animals that you appreciate for their affinities to your sign and the pets that you as an Arian can easily love and live with; the ways in which you need to take care of your body, and how your health and well-being may be affected by the fact that you were born under Aries.*

The fascinating range of this Sun Sign Companion *explains your temperament, your actions and the ways you live your life in zodiacal terms. You are a born leader and your special element – Arian fire – makes you enterprising and energetic; your planetary ruler Mars, the god of war, also gives you a particular dynamism. You have singular connections with the powers of the Earth itself – its gemstones, metals and crystals. And your zodiacal profile is underlined by your Arian connections to the ancient and mysterious arts of the Runes and the Tarot.*

This book provides you with the intriguing mosaic of influences, interests and attributes that build into the total picture of yourself as an Arian. More than any other zodiacal guide, your Sun Sign Companion *reveals to you the inherent fun and enjoyment of life under Aries.*

A R I E S

THE ZODIAC

hen the ancient astrologers studied the sky at night, they tracked the obvious motion and changing shape of the Moon, but noted two other phenomena: the frosty grandeur of the fixed stars and the different movements of the five observable planets. Mercury, Venus, Mars, Jupiter and Saturn moved and weaved about the night sky in repeating patterns, always within the same narrow strip of the heavens. And in the day time, the Sun could be seen progressing along the centre of this strip on its apparent orbit. Most of the action, celestially speaking, appeared to take place in a restricted

heavenly corridor. Astronomers and astrologers therefore gave priority to this ribbon of sky, and noted what else appeared in it.

Sharing the strip were twelve fixed star constellations, known from ancient times. They were Aries the Ram, Taurus the Bull, Gemini the Twins, Cancer the Crab, Leo the Lion, Virgo the Virgin, Libra the Balance, Scorpius the Scorpion, Sagittarius the Archer, Capricornus the Goat, Aquarius the Water Carrier and Pisces the Fishes. As most of the constellations are named after sentient creatures, the Greeks called this band of sky the zodiac, from their word meaning images of animals or living beings.

In astronomical terms, the constellations take up varying amounts of sky and exhibit different degrees of brightness. Astrologically, they are assigned equal prominence and importance, and are given equal 30-degree arcs of the celestial band. These are the signs of the zodiac, and the starting point on the celestial circle is 0 degrees Aries, which was the point of the vernal equinox over 4000 years ago when the zodiac was established.

The celestial jostling along the zodiacal corridor is explained by the fact that the planets orbit the Sun roughly in the same plane. Imagine yourself at the centre of a race track, timing a group of runners as they lap the circuit, each one running at a different pace and in a different lane. Soon you would be able to predict when each one would pass you, especially if you noted down landmarks along the spectator stands behind the runners.

In the same way, astrologers pinpoint the position and motion of any planet, using the zodiac band as a reference grid. Interpretation of the effects of planetary power filtered through the zodiac grid is the enduring fascination of astrology. The planets are extremely powerful, as signified by their having been awarded the names and attributes of the gods.

ZODIACAL INFLUENCES

our sun sign is the zodiac sign that the Sun, the most powerful of the heavenly bodies, appears to be passing through from our viewpoint on Earth at the time of your birth. It takes the Sun one year to progress through all the signs, and it is the Sun's huge power, filtered through each sign in turn, that etches the broad character templates of each sign. Over the centuries, each sign has acquired its own repertory of characteristics and personality traits, a seamless blend of archetypal myth and particular observation. So now we can talk about, say, a 'typical Arian' with the expectation that others will know what we mean. However, fine tuning and modification of the individual personality are dictated by two conditions at the time of birth – the positions of the Moon and planets in the zodiac and the nature of the ascendant, the sign rising on the eastern horizon at the moment of birth.

The Earth spins counter-clockwise daily on its axis, but to us it appears that the Sun, stars and planets wheel overhead from east to west. Within this framework, the zodiac passing overhead carries with it one sign every two hours; therefore the degree of the ascendant changes likewise, which explains why two people born on the same day can have such varying personalities. The influence of the ascending sign, and any planet positioned in it, has a strong bearing on the formation of the personality. An Arian with Pisces in the ascendant is quite a different kettle of fish to one with Capricorn ascending.

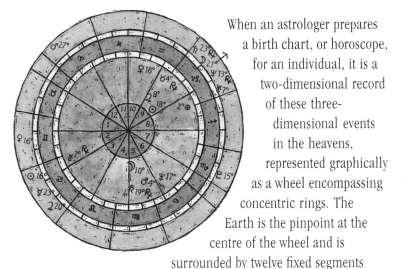

When an astrologer prepares a birth chart, or horoscope, for an individual, it is a two-dimensional record of these three-dimensional events in the heavens, represented graphically as a wheel encompassing concentric rings. The Earth is the pinpoint at the centre of the wheel and is surrounded by twelve fixed segments representing the zodiacal Houses, the areas of life in which planetary influences will manifest themselves. The outer circle of the chart represents the moving zodiacal corridor, divided into its twelve segments – the signs of the zodiac.

The predictability of the planets' movements has enabled astrologers to create tables, known as Ephemerides, of the planetary positions past, present and future. Once the positions of the Sun, Moon and planets have been established for a specific time, and a particular subject, the astrologer can assess and interpret what effects the planets will have, how they will enhance, diminish or frustrate each other's powers, and which areas of the subject's life will come under their particular influences. And all of this information is blended with the astrologer's understanding of the sun sign personality, the broad framework of individuality in zodiacal terms.

THE ARIES PERSONALITY

ries is the first sign of the zodiac, and coming first is the very essence of Aries. Intrepid, adventurous, energetic, outgoing, enthusiastic and impulsive, Arians are born leaders, eager to break new ground, unafraid to take risks, always ready to boldly go where others dare not, supremely confident in the rightness of their first response. Arians rarely look before they leap, and often rely on the inspiration of the moment to see things through.

Everything is done at a headlong pace: Arians hurl themselves into their work (often running two or three jobs at a time), their play (they excel at competitive sports) and their relationships (if anyone is going to fall wildly in love at first sight, it is Aries). Arians thrive on challenge, freedom to make their own policy and the chance to win. Whatever they do in life, they must be in charge and at the forefront of the action – deskbound routine and paper-shuffling douse the pioneering flame. Aries's leisure hours are crowded with hobbies that yield instant results – action painting rather than needlepoint – but Arians rarely stick with anything long enough to develop their talents.

In love, Aries is ardent, passionate, possessive and faithful – until the Arian loses that loving feeling, which can disappear as suddenly as it came. The broken hearts that litter their trail are a puzzle to Arians; being self-oriented, they are moved only by their own feelings. Empathy is an enigma to them, and seeing things from another's viewpoint is virtually impossible.

Aries ♈
Orbis Regens
Mars ➤ ☉ ➤
Signum Obstans
Libra ♎

THE PLANETARY RULER

ncient astrologers named the five planets they could see in the night sky after the five most powerful classical gods; naturally, the planets took on the attributes and associations of the gods, and a pleasingly symmetrical system was devised to distribute this planetary power throughout the zodiac.

The Sun and Moon, being the most dazzling lights, ruled one sun sign each (Leo and Cancer). The remaining ten signs managed under the shared patronage of the five planets. Mercury presided over Gemini and Virgo, Venus over Taurus and Libra, Mars over Aries and Scorpio, Jupiter over Sagittarius and Pisces, and Saturn over Aquarius and Capricorn.

When more planets were discovered after the invention of the telescope in 1610, a reshuffle became necessary. Uranus

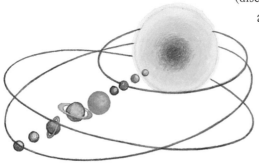
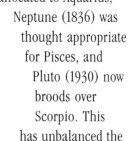

(discovered in 1781) was allocated to Aquarius, Neptune (1836) was thought appropriate for Pisces, and Pluto (1930) now broods over Scorpio. This has unbalanced the symmetry: the search is on for other planets to share the burden with Venus and Mercury. Indeed, the asteroid Chiron, discovered in 1977 looping the void between Saturn and Uranus, is considered by some astrologers to be the suitable governor of Virgo.

The planetary power associated with Aries comes from Mars, the warrior of the stars. Mars represents energy and enterprise, initiative and enthusiasm; it is quick, assertive, decisive and

restless, encouraging the urge to cut a dash, preferably single-handed. On the positive side, it promotes courage, endurance, physical activity, zest for life and the will to overcome obstacles and thrust on to success. Adversely, it can create a quarrelsome, reckless and disruptive environment, unnecessary violence and aggression.

Astronomically, Mars is the fourth planet in the solar system, just over half the size of Earth. It is easily visible to the naked eye, glowering redly in the heavens, and has two irregular, heavily cratered moons, Phobos and Deimos (Fear and Terror). Mars takes just over two-and-a-half years to orbit the Sun and work its way around the zodiac, spending just over two months in each sign.

In classical mythology, Mars is an uncomplicated, manly deity, the god of war. Mars is the Roman name for the Greek Ares, son of Zeus and Hera and consort of the goddess of love, Venus Aphrodite.

PATTERNS IN THE STARS

tar pictures, or constellations, are formed in the eye of the beholder. What we see as a neighbourly cluster is usually an optical illusion, the stars in the group being many light years apart. Even so, the urge to impose a friendly pattern on the frosty immensity of the night sky, to link the stars with the myths and legends on earth, has been irresistible to all cultures. Different cultures make out different pictures, and the results are sometimes inscrutable – searching for Leo, say, you will look in vain for the shape of a lion pricked out in stars against the dark backcloth of the night sky.

The zodiac constellations were among the first to be made out, as they were the main star groups that formed the background to the moving planets, providing a useful reference grid to plot planetary movements. These gave their names to the signs of the zodiac, although they spread unevenly across the sky and are not

tidily confined to the equal 30-degree segments of the imaginary zodiac band. Most stars are known by their Arabic names, and the star that shone brightest in each constellation when Arabic astrologers first compiled their star catalogues was designated its alpha.

The constellation that gave its name to the first sign of the zodiac is the northern star group Aries the Ram, a modest string of stars slung below the long rope of Andromeda. The three most distinctive stars are Hamal, the orange-coloured alpha visible to the naked eye, Sheratan and Mesartim. When the zodiac was being drawn up, over 4000 years ago, Aries was the constellation seen behind the Sun at the point of the spring equinox. Scholars throughout the civilized world fixed on this as the beginning of the zodiac year, and Aries became the first sign. The positions of the star groups as seen from Earth have been changing gradually over the centuries, and today the constellation behind the Sun at the spring equinox is Aquarius. But Aries is still considered to be the first sign as, typically, Aries will never willingly cede pole position.

Aries is the starry image of the mythical winged ram with the golden fleece, dispatched to Boetia by Zeus to save the youth Phrixus and his sister Helle from grisly death by sacrifice. Once rescued, and in spite of his sister falling from the ram's back into the part of the Ionian sea now called the Hellespont, Phrixus sacrificed the ram to Zeus. The glittering fleece, a much sought-after treasure, was sent to Colchis where it hung from an oak tree in the Grove of Ares, the god of war. It was later stolen by the hero Jason, to whom it brought nothing but trouble.

THE ATTRACTION OF OPPOSITES

In astrology the term polarity is used to describe the strong complementary relationship between signs that are exactly opposite each other on the zodiac circle, 180 degrees or six signs apart. These signs share the same gender – masculine or feminine – and the same quality – cardinal, fixed or mutable – and so share the ways they look at the world and shape their energy. Characteristics and interests complement each other or harmonize on different scales.

Relationships between polar signs are often very satisfying and fruitful, especially in the context of work. A clue to this affinity lies with the elements governed by each sign. The mathematics of polarity mean that earth signs oppose only water signs, and that fire opposes only air. Fire and air signs therefore encourage and inspire each other – fire cannot burn without air and air needs heat to rise. Earth and water signs conspire together creatively – earth without water is unfruitful, water unconfined by earth wastes

its energy in diffusion – and together they make mud, rich material for any creative process.

Six signs away from headstrong Aries, the leader of the pack who makes decisions at the snap of a finger, we find well-mannered, well-balanced, harmonious Libra, the diplomat of the zodiac. Scrupulous Libra weighs up the pros and cons and takes all viewpoints into consideration. The Libran ability to sit almost forever on the fence must be torture to Aries, who prefers to charge right through it headfirst.

Below the surface, however, a shared and complementary shaping energy is at work, the cardinal energy of creation. Aries and Libra preside over momentous times of the year, the spring and autumn equinoxes, when the Sun makes its decisive move from one hemisphere to the other, a time of new beginnings. Aries, the fire sign, burns with a hard, gem-like flame, intent on getting the individual show on the road. Libra, the air  sign, fans out its creative energy to include as many people as possible. Libra's gentle but determined energy diffraction prevents the intense Arian energy from burning so fiercely that it destroys itself and all around it.

The complementary aspect of polarity is also seen in the characteristics traditionally associated with the two signs. Both are keen to promote action to an end, but by their own instinctive methods – Aries by rushing out and doing it in person; Libra by bringing people together and persuading them to work together. Aries galvanizes the individual; Libra integrates the individual into society.

THE SYMBOLS OF THE ZODIAC

ver since astrology began, there has been a kind of astrological shorthand, a set of symbols or ideograms called glyphs. Glyphs make the language of astrology universal and available to people who have no literary tradition. They also make it a lot easier to draw up a birthchart, a convenient form of notation, especially when planets are clustered in one area of the chart.

Each of the zodiac signs has its own glyph, as do the planets. They have evolved over centuries, and so are now freighted with symbolism, not simply convenient codes.

Today, the glyph for Aries is recognizably a pair of curving ram's horns. Early Egyptians adopted something shaped like a hatchet; the Ram was considered an incarnation of the mighty sun god Amon-Ra, to whom axes were sacred. The Greek symbol looked like a small snake rearing

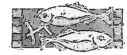

up on its tail – or a tiny sprouting seed. Medieval astrologers had two versions, one an ornate L-shape, the other a prototype of the modern glyph.

There is a special fascination in studying the glyphs to see what other symbolism may be contained within them – the Aries glyph could be seen as a sprouting plant, thrusting up through the cold soil towards warmth and light. It resembles gamma, the third letter of the Greek alphabet, which also signifies conjunction. Aries begins at the point of the vernal equinox, when the Sun's apparent path crosses the celestial equator.

The planets also have their glyphs, and the Mars symbol is familiar to all students of biology. It is the symbol of maleness, a circle with an arrow thrusting outward from it.

THE HOUSE OF ARIES

he twelve Houses of the zodiac are an intellectual concept, not a physical reality, an expression of all the aspects of human life and experience, from the self to the infinite. Each is associated with a sign of the zodiac, sharing its planetary ruler and elemental energy. However, the Houses are fixed and constant – they are represented

by the central numbered segments on a birth chart – and the signs and planets pass through them. They are the channels through which planetary and zodiacal energies flow and they indicate which area of life is the focus of particular zodiacal influence at any one time.

Aries, being first in everything, is associated with the First House, which is also overseen by Aries's planetary ruler, Mars. Like Aries, it is infused with fire energy, which means that it concerns character, personality and individual expression. In particular, the First House is concerned with the ego, the self in the world, the personality, physical build and appearance, disposition and constitution.

The First House is also the home of the ascendant, the sign rising over the eastern horizon at the time of birth. The sign and

planets occupying the house are very important in the formation of a person's basic personality and may extensively modify the broad characteristics laid down by the sun sign. So if you don't consider yourself to be a typical Arian, take a look at your rising sign and the planets, if any, that may be occupying your First House.

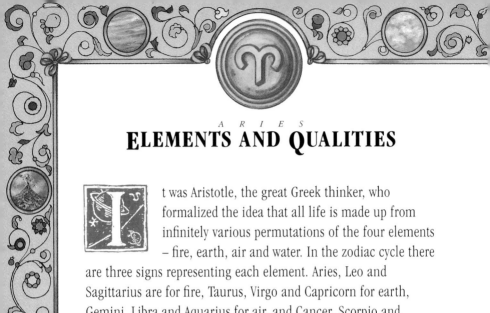

ELEMENTS AND QUALITIES

t was Aristotle, the great Greek thinker, who formalized the idea that all life is made up from infinitely various permutations of the four elements – fire, earth, air and water. In the zodiac cycle there are three signs representing each element. Aries, Leo and Sagittarius are for fire, Taurus, Virgo and Capricorn for earth, Gemini, Libra and Aquarius for air, and Cancer, Scorpio and Pisces for water.

However, in each case, the element is filtered through a different kind, or quality, of energy field; cardinal, fixed and mutable (or transforming). Aries, Cancer, Libra and Capricorn are cardinal; Taurus, Leo, Scorpio and Aquarius are fixed; Gemini, Virgo, Sagittarius and Pisces are mutable. Each sign is a unique manifestation of one element and one quality of energy.

Fire is the Aries element: glorious and terrifying, life-affirming and greedy for life, at once the purifier and the destroyer. This is the light of the gods, energy snatched from the Sun itself, stolen for humanity by Prometheus (who might be claimed by Arians as one of their own). It is the element that brought us civilization, and the ability to destroy it; the element capable of warming your slippers, or burning your house down.

Arians are very attracted to fire; watch them tending their barbecues or tinkering with their internal combustion engines. Firefighting is a supremely Arian career choice, and the all-time hero for Arians must be Red Adair, the oil-rig fire supremo.

Aries fire erupts through cardinal energy. Cardinal people are natural leaders because they are an ever-renewable source of their own energy, whatever its kind. As a fire cardinal, Aries is almost unstoppable. Think of a volcano, an awesome spew of fire, fuelled by a bottomless pit of molten magma: it is an irresistible force of nature at once destructive and productive – for lava cools to produce the most fertile soil in the world.

THE ZODIAC GARDEN

n Arian running through the park has no time to stand and stare. Not one to gaze at nature's wonders, Aries patronizes tough, self-made plants, the thistles and thorn trees that are unafraid to sprout in hostile surroundings. Bare heathland with a fringe of gorse and furze bushes or a forest of tough conifers struggling fiercely for their share of the light makes a suitable landscape background for Arian action.

Nor would any Arian win the Green Fingers award; they lack the nurturing touch. You won't find them hovering over shy seedlings or humming to tender tendrils. By the time the plant blossoms, Aries has moved on. To share the Arian home or backyard, plants must be tough. Nasturtiums – resilient, pungent and fiery – will survive in a neglected Arian window box (Aries loved making the box but soon lost interest in the slow growth of the tiny plants). Don't even think about giving houseplants to an Arian, except perhaps the indestructible aspidistra, veteran of many inhospitable sites – not for nothing is it called the cast-iron plant.

Aries as a gardener is best confined to the toolshed, enthusiastically maintaining the lawnmower, honing the blades of the hedge-trimmer into lethal weapons, rust-proofing the hoes, spades and trowels. Arians can also build the best bonfires in town. Otherwise, it would probably be kinder to pave the garden over and focus on an elaborate barbecue. However, ardent Arians will love to woo their latest flame under a bower of sweet-smelling, climbing honeysuckle – but will equally enjoy hacking back over-enthusiastic plant growth using state-of-the-art garden shears.

ASTROLOGY AND THE ARK

he word zodiac comes from the Greek word for living creatures, and the many of the signs are symbolized by animals. Aries is represented by the Ram, a gloriously potent image full of strength, sexual energy and self-importance. Unsurprisingly, Aries the sign is particularly associated with sheep, specifically rams.

Sheep, woolly-minded woolbearers, do not have the dynamism of Aries, but rams are a different matter. Every ram wants to be the leader of his pack, energetically head-butting his way through life, joyfully exercising *droit de seigneur* whenever he can, always aiming to be first in his field.

As Aries is such a self-oriented sign, it does not have much time for the rest of the animal kingdom. Pets are not a good idea. Arians would rather tinker with a machine – machines don't need regular feeding, don't pine away from neglect, nor take up valuable activity time. Any animal in an Arian home will have to be able to hold its own – maybe a hardboiled, self-feeding older cat, or a large, indestructible dog which can double as a status symbol and exercise machine.

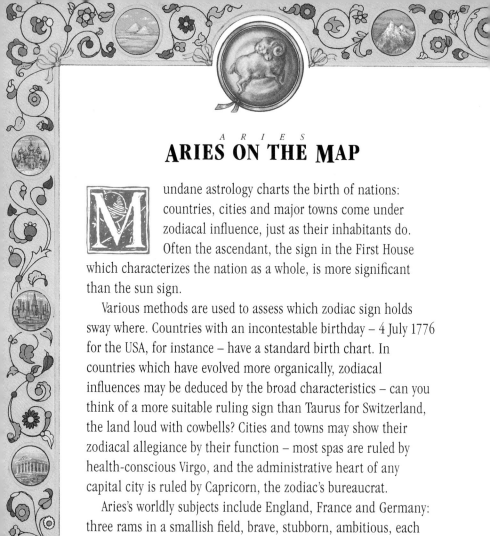

ARIES ON THE MAP

Mundane astrology charts the birth of nations: countries, cities and major towns come under zodiacal influence, just as their inhabitants do. Often the ascendant, the sign in the First House which characterizes the nation as a whole, is more significant than the sun sign.

Various methods are used to assess which zodiac sign holds sway where. Countries with an incontestable birthday – 4 July 1776 for the USA, for instance – have a standard birth chart. In countries which have evolved more organically, zodiacal influences may be deduced by the broad characteristics – can you think of a more suitable ruling sign than Taurus for Switzerland, the land loud with cowbells? Cities and towns may show their zodiacal allegiance by their function – most spas are ruled by health-conscious Virgo, and the administrative heart of any capital city is ruled by Capricorn, the zodiac's bureaucrat.

Aries's worldly subjects include England, France and Germany: three rams in a smallish field, brave, stubborn, ambitious, each convinced of its superiority, none keen on compromise. England's birth chart, drawn up for noon on Christmas Day 1066, the moment of William the Conqueror's coronation, shows Aries at 22 degrees in the ascendant. Other Arian countries are Syria, Poland and Denmark (remember the Vikings and their ram's-horn drinking cups).

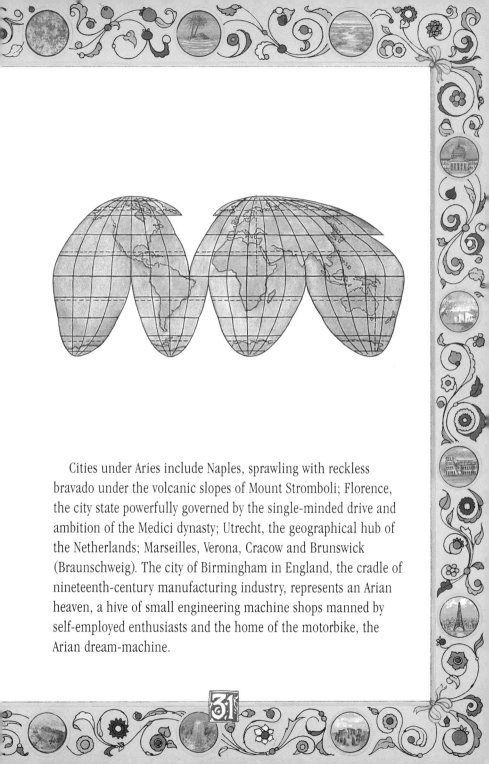

Cities under Aries include Naples, sprawling with reckless bravado under the volcanic slopes of Mount Stromboli; Florence, the city state powerfully governed by the single-minded drive and ambition of the Medici dynasty; Utrecht, the geographical hub of the Netherlands; Marseilles, Verona, Cracow and Brunswick (Braunschweig). The city of Birmingham in England, the cradle of nineteenth-century manufacturing industry, represents an Arian heaven, a hive of small engineering machine shops manned by self-employed enthusiasts and the home of the motorbike, the Arian dream-machine.

EARTH'S BOUNTY

ood plants associated with hasty Aries have to be good tempered, hardy and able more or less to grow themselves. Leeks and onions, fiery-tasting yet down to earth, with high yield for little effort, available all year round – even growing wild for Aries on the move – are ideal. They also clear the blood, and plenty of healthy flowing red blood is essential to Aries. Hops are another Arian form of growth - and beer is ready to drink so much more quickly than wine.

Although not ruled by Aries, tomatoes are very Arian; not only are they red, Aries's own colour, they also contain lots of potassium phosphate, the mineral salt that combats depression. Arians may be prey to despondency when they cannot do things their way. Tomatoes were once known as love-apples, considered to be blood-stirringly aphrodisiac, just the thing for ardent Aries. And according to macrobiotic dietary theory, tomatoes are very *yang*, that is, replete with the male principle.

Arian food is simple and unsophisticated; plenty of red meat is favourite. Subtle saucery

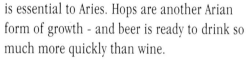

and finesse with garnishes are not for Aries, but this does not mean bland eating. Entertain your Arian dinner guests with cold beef with plenty of mustard, boiled lamb with caper sauce, anything with cayenne pepper – for its fiery taste and gorgeous colour.

Neither do Arians like to loll in chic eateries: when they eat out, they eat out. The barbecue is the quintessence of Aries; it offers total control – not only can Arians cook the food themselves, they can even build the barbecue – and it mingles metal, fire and a frisson of adventure in an intoxicating Arian cocktail.

A HEAVENLY HERBAL

 erbs and the heavens have been linked forever; for many centuries, herbs were the only medicine, and the gathering and application of them were guided by the planets. Doctors would learn the rudiments of astrology as a matter of course – Hippocrates claimed that 'a physician without a knowledge of astrology had no right to call himself a physician'.

Healing plants and their ruling planets were often linked via the elements – fire, water, air and earth. Mars, for example, a hot fiery planet, self-evidently rules over hot, fiery plants such as mustard. Herbs that cure the ills of particular parts of the body are ruled by the planet that governs that part of the body. Plants are also assigned according to what they look like. For example,

walnuts, which look like tiny models of the brain, are ruled by
Mercury, the planet which rules the brain.

All herbs are more effective if they are gathered on a day ruled
by their patron planet, especially at dawn, when they are fat with
sap drawn up by the beams of the Moon, or at dusk, after a day
basking in the strengthening rays of the Sun.

Arian herbs either reflect the fiery temperament of their ruler
Mars, or respond to the above-average need for first-aid remedies.
For a sign that likes it hot, mustard, cayenne pepper and capers
are natural complements – and mustard makes a useful plaster.
Arnica is balm to the bruise-mottled Arian, and is good for some
sorts of headache. Bryony is effective against muscle cramps
induced by Martian over-enthusiasm (Mars rules the muscular
system). Crowfoot helps to draw blisters (after all day on the move)
and rhubarb, the mild purgative, helps to rebalance the body's
water system, which is sometimes out of line in Aries.

THE CELESTIAL BODY

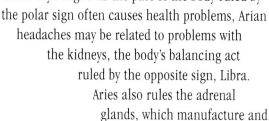

ach part of the body comes under the influence of a different zodiac sign. Appropriately for headfirst, headstrong Aries, the part of the body ruled by the first sign of the zodiac is the head. Arians may often complain of headaches – or, mysteriously, never have them, not even after the hardest day's night. As the part of the body ruled by the polar sign often causes health problems, Arian headaches may be related to problems with the kidneys, the body's balancing act ruled by the opposite sign, Libra. Aries also rules the adrenal glands, which manufacture and

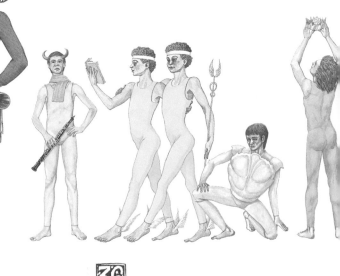

pump out the adrenalin that fuels most Arian enterprise. All that energy and dash results in an above average crop of cuts and bruises, especially cuts, and the Arian first-aid box may need to be equipped with industrial-sized packs of plasters and bandages.

The planets are thought to govern body systems and Aries's ruler, Mars, is associated with the muscular system, the urogenital system and the gonads (ovaries and testes), which helps to explain Aries's enthusiastic lust for life.

Arians are extraordinarily bump-prone, and should try not to live all their lives in the fast lane. They must also beware of flourishing their carving knives or metalworking tools too carelessly. After a typically action-packed day, peppermint oil is soothing and cool to hot and bothered Arians, used as a massage oil or in a simple smelling-bottle. For the head and face, gentle rose oil is luxurious as an all-over facial massage.

THE STARS AND THE STONES

Runes are a code, secret keys to the different facets of the whole interconnecting universe. Originated by the Germanic nomads who wandered the plains of northern Italy some 500 years before Christ, this compact and portable form of magic crossed the Alps and spread throughout northern Europe and Scandinavia. The twenty-four 'letters' of the *futharc* (an acronym of the first six letters of the runic alphabet) were used by the pragmatic Germans as a straightforward recording medium, as well as a shortcut to tapping the secrets of the universe. Each rune is a powerpacked symbol of one aspect of existence – for example, the fourth rune *As* means ash tree, but also signifies the tree of the world, the divine force that controls the cosmic order.

When the runes are cast, they combine, and the trained runemaster can read what has been, what is, and what influences are shaping future events. Authentic ancient runes, the portable arkana, were carved or painted on fresh-cut fruitwood and cast onto a white cloth for divination, but pebble or stone runes work just as well. Everyone should make their own runes – they have personal power, and they are free.

Runic astrology divides the sky into twenty-four segments, or seles, which correspond with the futharc. The seles modify the expression of planetary energy as each planet passes through them. The planets carry the attributes of the northern gods, and these too have runic associations.

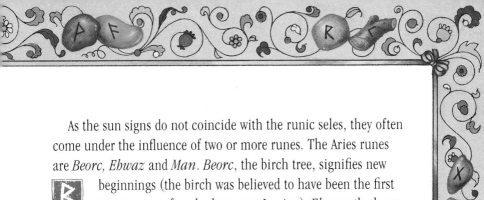

As the sun signs do not coincide with the runic seles, they often come under the influence of two or more runes. The Aries runes are *Beorc, Ehwaz* and *Man*. *Beorc*, the birch tree, signifies new

beginnings (the birch was believed to have been the first tree to grow after the last great Ice Age). *Ehwaz*, the horse,

is energy incarnate, exhilarating forward motion, a primal force that can be used for good or evil (a horse can also

bolt). *Man* is the self, the whole human being. The runic image of Aries – self in the saddle, courageous and reckless, charging full tilt, scornful of hazards, determined to finish the journey – is remarkably similar to the zodiacal profile.

Tir is the rune associated with Aries's ruler Mars, whose northern equivalent is the warrior sky god Tyr. *Tir* signifies directed energy, justified assertion, the aim and will to succeed.

> *These be the book runes*
> *And the runes of good help*
> *And all the taboo runes*
> *And the runes of much might.*

from *The Edda*

ZODIAC TREASURE

he zodiac treasure hoard may overflow with gorgeous gems, but it is guarded by grumpy and confused dragons, who squabble among themselves and cannot agree on which stone best fits which sign. However, the beguiling idea of a jewelled girdle encircling the zodiac is an ancient one, and may even be based on the twelve gemstones, one for each of the tribes of Israel, set on the breastplate of the Jewish high priests of biblical times. Medieval

astrologers felt reasonably sure of their ground and listed the gems as follows, in zodiacal order: bloodstone, sapphire, agate, emerald, onyx, carnelian, chrysolite, aquamarine, topaz, ruby, garnet and amethyst. Catherine de Medici, the original power-dresser, was rumoured to possess a glittering belt of zodiacal gems.

As there is no real concensus in the matter, a new approach is needed. Consideration of the colour and characteristics traditionally attributed to each sun sign may lead to a satisfying match of sign with stone.

Red is the unmistakable Arian colour: red for war, red for blood and for revolution, and the danger of red alert. Perhaps Arians should go for rubies: the Sun is exalted – that is, extra-powerful – in Aries, and rubies are traditionally associated with the Sun. Second choice could be the bloodstone, reputed to be able to prevent nosebleeds and staunch the flow of blood, very useful for the accident-prone Aries. But headstrong Aries needs something tougher – in fact, the toughest gemstone in the treasure chest, the diamond.

Diamonds are not only forever, and a girl's best friend, they are indisputably Arian. They glitter like liquid fire in the light, they make an incisive cutting edge, and they are varieties of carbon, the fuel that feeds fire and life. Used as healing crystals, they can purify the body and stimulate courage. Fortunately for their friends, Arians are not greedy, and a rope of diamanté chunks will be joyfully accepted if the real thing is out of reach.

EARTH'S HIDDEN POWER

eneath the earth, in the realm of Pluto, lie the solidified energies, metals and crystals that hum with compacted potency.

Aries's metal is iron, tough and valiant, made for action not decoration, the metal that confounds the Devil, the metal of the fighting man – such as England's Iron Duke, Wellington. Iron yields to nothing except the superior force of that other supremely Arian element, fire. As the main component of steel, iron is the stuff of swords, ploughshares and the sharp-edged knives that so fascinate Arians. The Aries kitchen will contain a massive wooden block bristling with carbon steel knives for every possible culinary need. Metalwork is a major Arian hobby, and tinkering with a motorbike, the iron steed – usually on the kitchen table – is Aries's very heaven.

Crystals are chemical elements compressed over millenia into dense, solid form, storehouses of electromagnetic energy. The Aries crystal is quartz, a plain, no-nonsense crystal intended for action not ornament. Like iron it is inexpensive and easily available, and like iron it has extraordinary powers. Quartz crystal is considered to be the boss, the top of the crystal hierarchy. It works on the whole person, receiving, storing, activating and amplifying the energies its owner pours into it. It stimulates brain activity, enhances the activities of the body systems and combats negativity in thought and deed. This is the crystal that unleashes the boundless Arian energy and promotes the larger-than-life image of Mars subjects. Mars's own crystals are citrine quartz, the detoxifier and enemy to self-destruction, and agate (a form of chalcedony), for strength and courage in body and mind.

Each crystal is an individual, and you must always choose your own. Take your time, pick up those that attract you and handle them gently; you will eventually find the one that uniquely suits you.

ARIES ON THE CARDS

ometimes called the Devil's Picture Book, the tarot was probably created in the twelfth century, but its origins are suitably shrouded in secrecy. There are seventy-eight cards: twenty-two in the Major Arcana, a gallery of enigmatic archetypal images from the Fool via the Wheel of Fortune to the World; and fifty-six in the Minor Arcana, divided into four suits – coins, cups, swords and batons (or wands).

Tarot cards, being one of the ways to explore the human psyche, have an affinity with the zodiac sun signs. Cards from the Major Arcana and the picture cards from the Minor Arcana are associated with specific signs. If two cards are assigned, they should be considered together.

To Aries falls the Fool – a singular card in the pack, the card that has no number. The Fool is Everyman, the unmatured personality,

striding out confidently into the world, laughing carelessly (or dementedly in some cases), oblivious to hazards. The Arian representative in the Minor Arcana is the King of Swords, a powerful and authoritative figure with an unsheathed sword, ever

ready for action – energetic, determined, in charge, unchallengeable (he is the king), living for the moment – but also reckless, impulsive and hasty.

Aries's ruler Mars is associated with the Emperor, the symbol of the active male principle, earthly power, legitimized aggression, creative assertion. A second influence comes from the Tower, symbolic of shattering, the destruction of things, both good and evil. Risk-taking, accident-prone Aries will instantly recognize this card.

There are many ways to lay out the tarot cards for a reading, but a particularly zodiacal one is to place the significator (the card chosen to represent the questioner) in the centre and lay out the other cards in a circle, running anticlockwise and starting from the nine-o-clock position. This follows the layout of the astrological Houses, and the cards are interpreted in the context of the House in which they fall.

INDEX